Rookie Read-About™ Science

Please Don't Feed the Bears

By Allan Fowler

Images supplied by VALAN Photos

Consultants:
Robert L. Hillerich, Ph.D., Bowling Green
State University, Bowling Green, Ohio

Mary Nalbandian, Director of Science,
Chicago Public Schools, Chicago, Illinois

Fay Robinson, Child Development Specialist

 CHILDRENS PRESS®

CHICAGO

Series cover and interior design by Sara Shelton

Library of Congress Cataloging-in-Publication Data

Fowler, Allan.
    Please don't feed the bears / by Allan Fowler.
      p. cm. — (Rookie read-about science)
    Summary: A simple introduction to the physical characteristics,
habits, and natural environment of bears.
    ISBN 0-516-04916-X
    1. Bears—Juvenile literature. [1. Bears.] I. Title.
  II. Series: Fowler, Allan. Rookie read-about science.
QL737.C27F68 1991
599.74'446—dc20   91-3130
                                                 CIP
                                                 AC

    12 13 14 15 R 06 05 04

Where do you find bears ?

Most of them live in the woods.

6

A bear family's home,
or den, might be a cave

or a snow den,

or a hollow tree.

Bears love to eat.

That's why people say,
"I'm as hungry as a bear!"

Bears eat fruits and berries
and other plants.

They eat small animals and insects.

Some bears can snatch fish out of a stream with their paws.

Many bears spend the
winter sleeping inside their
dens.

Bear cubs are born in the winter.

When spring comes, the cubs finally leave the den and enjoy playing in the woods outside.

The bears you see most
often are called black bears.

The biggest bears are the ones called brown bears.

A grizzly is a kind of
brown bear.

Polar bears are white.

They live in the Arctic,
the land close to the
North Pole.

Their thick coats keep them warm when they swim in the icy waters.

Bears look funny when they stand on their hind legs, and when they do tricks in the circus.

But they are really wild animals.

So please don't ever, ever feed a bear—not in the zoo, not in the woods.

You could get hurt.

And the bear has enough to eat anyhow!

Words You Know

bears

black bears

brown bears

cubs

grizzly bears

polar bears

dens

cave

hollow tree

snow den

The Arctic

Index

About the Author

Allan Fowler is a free-lance writer with a background in advertising. Born in New York, he lives in Chicago now and enjoys traveling.

Photo Credits